MUSIC by BLACK COMPOSERS

RACHEL BARTON PINE
FOUNDATION

VIOLIN VOLUME 1

Beginner to Elementary Level
For Violin with 2nd Violin or Piano Accompaniment

Table of Contents

Listen to free recordings and find more resources online at
www.musicbyblackcomposers.org/violin1

55371001

LudwigMasters PUBLICATIONS

FOREWORD

Music by Black Composers (MBC) is a groundbreaking effort that is poised to transform the impact and trajectory of violin repertoire. From a pedagogical standpoint, its contributions will utterly shift the viewpoint of teachers and students alike, offering a wide array of music by composers of African descent. Arguably as important is its value to the field as a whole: by creating a new avenue for rarely, if ever, heard voices, the canon will undoubtedly be enriched.

The collection offers a great deal of social value that goes beyond music education and pedagogical advancement. During a time that can be divisive, chaotic, and dissonant, MBC offers a rich array of perspectives for any teaching artists looking to nurture a connection between their craft and the lives of their young students who are growing up to become artist citizens. Normalizing the inclusion of composers of color for the next generation of teachers, students, and audiences is timely and laudable.

Beyond those valuable aspects, the carefully curated selections in the collection simply represent a great deal of artistic value and excellence. The variety of art music styles—such as French and English classical-period works, pieces featuring rhythms from West Africa, music from Latin America and the Caribbean, interpretations of late 19th/early 20th-century American vernaculars—offer an exhilarating learning opportunity that will greatly augment the learning experience of young people as well as professionals across cultural backgrounds. The project makes a special effort to seek out and include women composers, further emphasizing the importance of early role modeling. In fact, MBC's Violin Volume 1 is more diverse than any other historical or current pedagogical material available today.

I encourage our teaching community to take full advantage of this remarkable resource and fully explore the incredible offering made available through the work of the Rachel Barton Pine Foundation! I look forward to a time when the full MBC collection becomes a part of the standard teaching canon across the board.

—Aaron Dworkin
 Professor of Arts Leadership & Entrepreneurship
 School of Music, Theatre & Dance; University of Michigan
 Professor of Entrepreneurial Studies
 Stephen M. Ross School of Business; University of Michigan
 Founder & President, ArtsShare.com
 Founder, The Sphinx Organization
 Member, The National Council on the Arts
 MacArthur Fellow

INTRODUCTION

Welcome to the RBP Foundation's *Music by Black Composers* series for violin! After 15 years of work, we are so pleased to begin sharing this beautiful music and fascinating history with you.

This collection is intended for students of all races and ethnicities, for those studying privately or in a group setting, and for children and adult learners. It is not a stand-alone curriculum. Rather, our graded volumes are designed to enable everyone from beginners through Mendelssohn Concerto level to include works by Black composers in their studies. Each piece in Volume 1 has both a piano accompaniment and a second violin accompaniment. The second violin part may be played by the teacher in lessons or performances, by a more advanced student as chamber music, or used in a group violin class.

Even though this volume is limited to works by Black composers (as defined by the North American conception of racial categories), it represents a remarkable degree of diversity. It contains works by both men and women. Geographically, the composers come from North America (the United States), South America (Brazil), the Caribbean (Cuba, Puerto Rico), Europe (England, France, Switzerland), and Africa (Ghana, Nigeria). And historically, the repertoire spans four centuries—from the 1700s to the present.

This collection is also stylistically broad: 6/8 (Sancho), rhythms of two against three (Gotay, Kafui, Ogungbe), syncopation (Cook, Joplin), waltzes (Weston, White), dotted rhythms (Barès, Sancho, Wiggins), graceful classicism (Saint-Georges, Sancho), and lyrical melodies in major and minor keys (Gonzaga, Gutiérrez, Martin, Roldan). Many of these concepts are absent in most pedagogical materials at the elementary level. We have also carefully chosen each piece for its melodic appeal. For example, you can't hear the Sadoh and not have it in your ear for the rest of the day.

My hope is that, in part through exposure to this repertoire, current and future generations of performers, presenters and audience members will expect and demand that music on our concert stages be a full representation of the human experience.

I am deeply indebted to so many terrific people and organizations, without whom you would not be holding this volume. Thank you very much to my husband Greg who encouraged me to begin this journey and shares my passion for it; to my first partner in this project, the late Dr. Dominique-René de Lerma; to my current collaborator, Dr. Mark Clague of the University of Michigan; to all of our generous donors, without whom this idea would never have become reality; to our dedicated Board of Advisors, who have offered so much invaluable guidance along the way; to our wonderful researchers, past and present: Tania Tam, Suzanne Pekow, Jules Lai, Trevor Croxson, Elliott Powell, Rashida Black, Dr. Michael Mauskapf, Dr. Evan Ware, and Dr. Megan E. Hill; to our contributing writer Danielle Taylor and our arrangers Dr. Carlos Simon and David Bontemps; to the many libraries who provided us with materials and information, in particular the Center for Black Music Research at Columbia College, the Columbus Museum (Georgia), the Hogan Jazz Library at Tulane University, the Historic New Orleans Collection, and the Library of Congress; to my colleagues Terrance Gray, Isabelle Rozendaal, Allison Bengfort, and Hilary Butler, who helped review all 900+ pieces to make selections for this series; to Ed Kreitman, who helped with the final sequence and editing; to my daughter Sylvia who diligently practiced and performed these pieces with me; to Joe Galison, Lynne Latham, Bryan Bird, and the rest of the wonderful team at LudwigMasters; and to all of my friends from the Sphinx family, the Chicago Music Association, and the Chicago Symphony's African American Network for their ongoing support and encouragement.

I hope that this music and history will give you a deeper appreciation of the contributions that Black musicians have made and are making to classical music. As you learn and teach these pieces, please be sure to send us feedback! Contact information is on our website, www.musicbyblackcomposers.org.

Please be sure to tag us when you post videos ("Music by Black Composers - MBC" and "Rachel Barton Pine Foundation - RBPF" on Facebook, @MBComposers and @RBP_Foundation on Twitter, @MBComposers and @RBP_Foundation on Instagram, and our YouTube channels). Our hashtags for this music are #blackisclassical, #celebrateblackcomposers, #musicbyblackcomposers, and #expandthecanon.

I look forward to hearing from you. Happy practicing!

—Rachel Barton Pine
Chicago, September 2018

ABOUT MUSIC BY BLACK COMPOSERS

Music by Black Composers (MBC) was born from the realization that young musicians learning classical music seldom, if ever, have the opportunity to study and perform music written by Black composers. This omission silences a rich vein of musical creation from global cultural consciousness. The effects of this erasure are most serious for aspiring Black classical musicians. Without access to the historic narratives of Black composers, these young musicians struggle to become part of an art form in which they do not appear to belong. Many give up; many more do not even start. The ultimate result is a lack of diversity in our concert halls, both on stage as well as in the audience.

MBC tells a different story. With this published series, we are supplementing the current instrumental training methods with collections of music exclusively by Black composers from around the world. Each string instrument will the subject of multiple volumes, which are graded by difficulty from beginner to advanced concerto-level playing. We also intend to publish music for wind and brass instruments, band, orchestra, and chamber ensembles. In addition to making this repertoire available, our books educate through articles and interviews. Each volume includes biographies for every composer, features on Black classical music making throughout history, and profiles of Black role models in classical music, past and present.

MBC also develops other educational and informational resources for students, performers, and members of the broader community. We have created a coloring book that features 40 of the most important Black composers from the 18th-21st centuries, as well as a timeline poster that will feature more than 300 Black composers from around the world. We are also creating an online database which will provide information about works written by Black composers. Designed for use by students, teachers, performers, administrators, researchers, and librarians, it will contain facts about each composer and about individual pieces, information about where to find the music, links to recordings, and more. Other online resources include a bibliography of publications about Black classical music making, and a directory of living composers for those commissioning new works or simply seeking information.

Over recent years, many educational and performance organizations have helped the cause of diversity by providing the opportunity for aspiring young Black musicians to realize their dreams. We believe that our project represents the next step. By changing the story about the music of Black composers, we want to help children be able to dream their dreams in the first place, and for those dreams to resonate throughout our communities and beyond.

Learn more at www.musicbyblackcomposers.org.

CONTRIBUTOR BIOGRAPHIES

Rachel Barton Pine
Executive Editor and Music Editor

Heralded as a leading interpreter of the great classical masterworks, international concert violinist Rachel Barton Pine thrills audiences with her dazzling technique, lustrous tone and emotional honesty. With an infectious joy in music-making and a passion for connecting historical research to performance, Pine transforms audiences' experiences of classical music.

Pine has appeared as soloist with many of the world's most prestigious ensembles, including the Chicago and Vienna Symphonies, the Philadelphia Orchestra, the Royal Philharmonic, and Camerata Salzburg. Her festival appearances have included Marlboro, Wolf Trap, Vail, Ravinia, Davos, and Salzburg. She holds prizes from several of the world's leading competitions, including a gold medal at the 1992 J.S. Bach International Violin Competition in Leipzig, Germany.

In addition to Pine's recital programs, she regularly gives single evening performances of the six Bach Sonatas and Partitas, the 24 Paganini Caprices, and the complete Brahms Sonatas. The *Washington Post* called her recent Bach performance "...as astonishing and joyful a performance of all three sonatas and three partitas as I've ever heard."

She has worked with such renowned conductors as Zubin Mehta, Erich Leinsdorf, Neeme Järvi and Marin Alsop, and with such leading artists as Daniel Barenboim, Christoph Eschenbach, Christopher O'Riley, and William Warfield. She has collaborated with many contemporary composers including Augusta Read Thomas, John Corigliano, José Serebrier, and Mohammed Fairouz.

Pine has a prolific discography of 37 albums on the Avie, Cedille, Warner Classics, and Dorian labels. Her 2016 *Testament: Complete Sonatas and Partitas for Solo Violin by Johann Sebastian Bach* hit number one on the *Billboard* Classical chart. Her *Mozart: Complete Violin Concertos, Sinfonia Concertante* with Sir Neville Marriner and The Academy of St Martin in the Fields marked her Avie Records debut and charted at number three on the *Billboard* Traditional Classical Chart.

Pine began an exploration of beloved violin concertos and the concertos that inspired them with *Brahms and Joachim Violin Concertos*, recorded with the Chicago Symphony Orchestra and conductor Carlos Kalmar. Her *Beethoven & Clement Violin Concertos*, with The Royal Philharmonic conducted by José Serebrier, offered the world premiere recording of Clement's *D Major Violin Concerto*.

Her recording of *Violin Lullabies* debuted at number one on the *Billboard* classical chart. Her *Violin Concertos by Black Composers of the 18th and 19th Centuries* sheds light on four gifted musicians of African descent who made important contributions to European music in the 1700s and 1800s and was nominated for a National Public Radio Heritage Award.

In 2009, Carl Fischer published *The Rachel Barton Pine Collection*, earning her the distinction of being the only living artist and first woman to join great musicians like Fritz Kreisler and Jascha Heifetz in Carl Fischer's *Masters Collection* series. Pine is music advisor and editor of *Maud Powell Favorites*, the only published compilation of music dedicated to, commissioned by, or closely associated with the first native-born American violinist to achieve international recognition.

Pine collaborated with Carl Fischer on her *J.S. Bach: Six Sonatas and Partitas*, her *Violin Lullabies* companion scores of compositions featured on her *Violin Lullabies* album, and her Book 1 and Book 2 editions of *Franz Wohlfahrt Foundation Studies for the Violin*.

Her Rachel Barton Pine (RBP) Foundation assists young artists. The RBP Foundation recently received the donation of the Arkwright Lady Rebecca Sylvan Stradivarius of 1732 to pair with a worthy recipient through its thriving Instrument Loan Program. Other programs include Grants for Education and Career and Global HeartStrings (supporting musicians in developing countries), in addition to Music by Black Composers.

Pine performs on the 1742 Joseph Guarnerius del Gesu "ex-Bazzini, ex-Soldat" on lifetime loan from her anonymous patron.

Megan E. Hill, Ph.D.
Managing Editor, Head Researcher & Writer

Megan E. Hill, Ph.D. is an ethnomusicologist, educator, and music editor. Before becoming involved with Music by Black Composers, she completed a Ph.D. in Musicology with an Ethnomusicological Emphasis at the University of Michigan. While there, she was also assistant editor at the Gershwin Initiative, producing critical editions of the works of George and Ira Gershwin, where she worked on projects including *Porgy and Bess* and *An American in Paris*.

As an ethnomusicologist, Dr. Hill's area of specialization is in music in contemporary Japan, with a secondary specialization in American popular music. In her dissertation, "Asakusa Ondo: Soundscape, Agency, Montage, and Place in a Dynamic Tokyo Neighborhood" (2016), she offered a theoretical framework for analyzing and understanding the ways that people make sense of sound, music, and place in dense, diverse urban environments. She has broad research interests that intersect with issues of music, place, race, ethnicity, gender, sexuality, and other aspects of human identity and experience in everyday life.

Dr. Hill has presented her research at the 3rd International Council for Traditional Music Forum (Beijing, 2018), the Music Integration and Innovation Symposium (Beijing, 2018), the Society for Ethnomusicology's annual conference (Denver, 2016; Washington, DC, 2017), the Association for Asian Studies (Toronto, 2017), Stony Brook University's Periods and Waves Conference (2016), Boston University's Sound and Bodies in the World Conference (2015), and the Inter-Asia Popular Music Conference (Taiwan Normal University, 2012). She has been an invited guest lecturer for courses and symposia at the University of Michigan and the University of Toledo. She was the recipient of the inaugural William P. Malm Prize for Outstanding Student Writing (2010) from the Center for Japanese Studies at the University of Michigan, the Glenn McGeoch Memorial Scholarship in Musicology Pedagogy (2016) from the School of Music, Theatre & Dance at the University of Michigan, and the Louise E. Cuyler Prize in Musicology (2016) from the University of Michigan's Musicology Department. Her dissertation field research was supported by a Dissertation Fellowship (2011-2012) from the Japan Foundation.

Most recently, Dr. Hill was invited by the Chinese Music Culture Institute as a research scholar for the 2018 International Summer Institute in Beijing, China, where she carried out a research project on the soundscapes of the city of Beijing.

She is currently a Lecturer in Ethnomusicology at Western Michigan University where she teaches the undergraduate capstone music course on ethnomusicological theory and practice. She has a number of articles in progress for publication on such topics as the musical construction of place in a Tokyo neighborhood, a contemporary Japanese band's *glocalization* of a local folk song, the politics of gendered language in Japanese popular song, and the creative musical practice of a Japanese blues pianist in Chicago, Illinois.

Mark Clague, Ph.D.
Chief Advisor

Mark Clague, Ph.D. is an Associate Professor of Musicology, American Culture, and African American Studies at the University of Michigan School of Music, Theatre & Dance, where he also serves as Associate Dean of Academic and Student Affairs. While completing his Ph.D. in musicology at the University of Chicago, he took his first scholarly job as an editorial assistant and writer for the two-volume *International Dictionary of Black Composers*, working alongside Dr. Samuel Floyd.

Having published articles and spoken at national conferences on the music of Arthur Cunningham, Anthony Davis, Akin Euba, Jimi Hendrix, Wynton Marsalis, Herbert Mells, Ornette Coleman, and George Walker, Dr. Clague edited the Memoirs of Alton Augustus Adams, Sr., First Black Bandmaster of the United States Navy for publication in the African Diaspora Series of the University of California Press, and curated an Adams tribute concert in the Virgin Islands by the U.S. Navy Ceremonial Band. He has created editions of Adams's most famous marches: *The Virgin Islands March* and *The Governor's Own*. He also wrote the liner notes for Rachel Barton Pine's recording *Violin Concertos by Black Composers*

(Cedille Records, 1997) and her recent *Blues Dialogues* project (Cedille Records, 2018).

A specialist in American music research, Dr. Clague's other writings can be found in the *Journal of the Society for American Music, American Music, Black Music Research Journal, Opera Quarterly*, and books published by Oxford University Press, Rowman & Littlefield Education, and the University of California and Illinois Presses. He served as city and institutions editor for the *New Grove Dictionary of American Music, Second Edition*, and he is editor-in-chief of the *George and Ira Gershwin Critical Edition* and co-editor-in-chief of *Music of the United States of America*.

Dr. Clague's research on the U.S. national anthem has led to the publication of the *Star Spangled Songbook* (2015) and the double CD *Poets and Patriots: A Tuneful History of "The Star-Spangled Banner"* (2014). In 2013,

he spoke at Detroit's SphinxCon about the history of abolitionist lyrics for "The Star-Spangled Banner." He was awarded one of the inaugural NEH Public Scholar fellowships to complete a book on the two-hundred-year history of the song. His anthem research has appeared in the *Journal of the Society for American Music*, the *Choral Journal*, and Chorus America's *The Voice*, and has sparked collaborations with the Smithsonian Museum of American History, the Grammy Museum in Los Angeles, and in recital with baritone Thomas Hampson at the U.S. Library of Congress. He also helped create the Star Spangled Music Foundation, built the website starspangledmusic.org, and started an affiliated YouTube channel. Addressing a target audience of K–12 teachers and the general public, these online initiatives have received more than 600,000 visits. He has been a project advisor to the Rachel Barton Pine Foundation since 2008.

David Bontemps
Contributing Arranger

David Bontemps was born in Port-au-Prince, Haiti. His parents were music lovers and enrolled him in private piano lessons very early. Most of his training in piano performance and music theory was given by the renowned pianist-composer Serge Villedrouin. He has lived in Montreal since 2002.

Mr. Bontemps accompanied Chantal Lavigne, mezzo soprano, for the creation in 2005 of *Offrandes Vodouesques*, 24 melodies by the Haitian composer Werner Jaëgerhuber, recorded and released in 2007. With a grant from Canada Council for the Arts and Conseil des Arts et des Lettres du Québec, he released *Vibrations* (label Nuits D'Afrique) in 2012, a disc dedicated to his best piano works. Critically acclaimed, this opus was the *Magazine Audio* first choice for 2012 albums.

In 2006, Mr. Bontemps founded and directed the quintet Makaya for which he composes and arranges most of the titles. This group, winner of the bronze medal at the Syli d'Or of World Music Contest in 2007,

released its first independent album in May 2009. Thanks to this eponymic album, the quintet was nominated for the TD Grand Jazz Award at the International Jazz Festival of Montreal in 2010. With *Elements*, released in 2016 with a grant from the Conseil des arts et des lettres du Quebec, the quintet continues to collect enthusiasm, topping jazz and world airplays on IciMusique and CIBL radios, among best performances in the 2016 FIJM by Le Devoir, and the Vision Diversity and CIBL prizes.

In 2015, he composed and recorded the music of Through Positive Eyes – Haiti, UCLA, a project of 12 films to fight discrimination against people living with HIV. With his latest solo release, *Gede Nibo* (2017) he contributed to Haïti Piano Project, which brought a grand piano to Jacmel, Haiti, where a piano festival is now founded.

Carlos Simon, D.M.A.
Contributing Arranger

Dr. Carlos Simon is a versatile composer and arranger who combines the influences of jazz, gospel, and neo-romanticism.

His latest album, *My Ancestor's Gift*, was released on the Navona Records label in April 2018. As a part of the Sundance Institute, Simon was named as a Sundance Composer Fellow in 2018. His string quartet, *Elegy*,

honoring the lives of Trayvon Martin, Michael Brown, and Eric Garner, was recently performed at the Kennedy Center for the Mason Bates JFK Jukebox Series. With support from the US Embassy in Tokyo and US/Japan Foundation, Simon traveled with the Asia/America New Music Institute (AANMI) on a two-week tour of Japan in 2018 performing in temples and concert spaces in Japan including Suntory Hall in Tokyo, Japan. Other recent accolades include being a Composer Fellow at the Cabrillo Festival for Contemporary Music, winning the Underwood Emerging Composer Commission from the American Composers Orchestra in 2016, the prestigious Marvin Hamlisch Film Scoring Award in 2015, and the Presser Award from the Theodore Presser Foundation in 2015.

Recent commissions have come from Morehouse College celebrating its 150th founding anniversary, the University of Michigan Symphony band celebrating the university's 200th anniversary, Albany Symphony's Dogs of Desire (American Music Festival) as well as serving as the young composer-in-residence with the Detroit Chamber Strings and Winds in 2016. Simon's music has been performed by diverse prestigious artists and ensembles throughout the United States. His piece, *Let America Be America Again* (text by Langston Hughes), is scheduled to be featured in an upcoming PBS documentary chronicling the inaugural Gabriela Lena Frank Academy of Music. Acting as music director and keyboardist for Grammy-Award-winner

Jennifer Holliday, Simon has also performed with the Boston Pops Symphony, Jackson Symphony, and St. Louis Symphony. He has toured internationally with soul Grammy-nominated-artist Angie Stone, and performed throughout Europe, Africa, and Asia. He now serves as a member of the music faculty at Spelman College in Atlanta, Georgia.

Simon earned his D.M.A. at the University of Michigan, where he studied with Michael Daugherty and Evan Chambers. He has also received degrees from Georgia State University and Morehouse College. Additionally, he studied in Baden, Austria at the Hollywood Music Workshop with Conrad Pope and at New York University's Film Scoring Summer Workshop.

Simon is a member of many music organizations including ASCAP, where he was honored as one of the "Composers to Watch" in 2015. He is also an honorary member of Phi Mu Alpha Music Sinfonia Fraternity and a member of the National Association of Negro Musicians, Society of Composers International, and Pi Kappa Lambda Music Honor Society. His compositions have been published by the Gregorian Institute of America (GIA) Publications and Hal Leonard Publications.

Danielle Taylor, B.M., B.A.
Contributing Writer

Danielle Taylor is a violinist and violist from Oakland, CA. She began formal music study through a school music program in fourth grade, with informal music training from a young age through singing in church. Since her childhood introduction to classical music, Danielle has earned a BA in African American Studies and a BM in Violin Performance (Oberlin College and Conservatory) and is scheduled to complete a MM in Violin Performance (Northwestern University) in Winter 2019.

Danielle plans to continue her education by pursuing her Ph.D. in Music Education. Her many research interests include classical music performers and composers from the African diaspora, as well as investigating issues of race, place, and power in classical music performance and education in the U.S.

A passionate violin teacher, Danielle maintains a growing studio in Chicago. She has taught in many capacities, including as a public middle and high school music instructor, as well as working with the Oakland Youth Orchestra as a violin Sectional Coach.

She has also worked in several Chicago area music programs, including for the Young Music Scholars program of the Midwest Young Artists Conservatory.

As an orchestral musician, Danielle has held a fellowship with the Grant Park Music Festival's Project Inclusion program and has also been a member of the Chicago Sinfonietta's Project Inclusion Ensemble. Danielle is a member of the Zafa Collective, a Chicago based New Music collective. Danielle is also the Artistic Director and violist for D-composed, a Chicago based chamber music series that celebrates and promotes musicians and composers of the African diaspora. D-composed launched its '18–'19 season as a selected participant in the prestigious Chicago Ideas Festival where they presented *D-compressed: A Chamber Music and Yoga Experience.*

BOARD OF ADVISORS and HONORARY BOARD MEMBERS

MBC's Board of Advisors

James Blachly • Orchestral Music by Black Composers, conductor
David Caines Burnett • violinist, violin teacher
Dr. Tanya L. Carey • cellist, cello professor, Suzuki teacher trainer
Aaron Dworkin • Sphinx Organization, University of Michigan
Anthony Elliot • cellist, cello professor
Robert Fisher • violist and violinist, strings teacher
Henry Fogel • Former President & CEO of the League of American Orchestras
Terrance Gray • violinist, conductor
Mariana Green • violinist, violin teacher
Sheila A. Jones • African American Network of the Chicago Symphony Orchestra
Lee Koonce • Gateways Music Festival
Edward Kreitman • Suzuki teacher trainer
Diane Monroe • violinist, composer
Michael Morgan • conductor
Toni-Marie Montgomery • Dean of the Bienen School of Music at Northwestern University
Lee Newcomer • Performers Music
Chi-chi Nwanoku OBE • Chineke!, double bassist
Dr. Fred "FredO" Onovwerosuoke • African Musical Arts, composer
Awadagin Pratt • pianist, piano professor
Dr. Rita Simó • People's Music School
Arnold Steinhardt • violinist, Guarneri Quartet, violin professor
Almita Vamos • violinist, violin professor
Mike Wright • music researcher, composer
Dr. Barbara Wright-Pryor • music writer, Past President of the Chicago Music Association
William J. Zick • AfriClassical.com

In Memoriam

Gilda Barston • cello teacher, Suzuki teacher trainer
Roque Cordero • composer
Dr. Dominique-René de Lerma • music researcher
Kermit Moore • cellist, cello teacher, composer, conductor
Helen Walker-Hill • pianist, music researcher

MBC's Honorary Board

Wilner Baptiste • Black Violin
Joshua Bell • violinist
Gretchen Carlson • television commentator
Billy Childs • pianist, composer
Stanley Clarke • jazz bassist, composer
Denyce Graves • mezzo-soprano
Wynton Marsalis • trumpeter, composer, Jazz at Lincoln Center
Chi-chi Nwanoku OBE • Chineke!, double bassist
Leslie Odom, Jr. • actor
Daniel Bernard Roumain • violinist, composer
Kevin Sylvester • Black Violin
André Watts • pianist, piano professor

Juwon Ogungbe

Juwon Ogungbe (b. 1961) is a composer, singer, musical director, educator, and instrumentalist. He was born in London, England to parents of Yoruba ethnic heritage from the West African country of Nigeria. When he was young, he was raised by English foster parents while his birth parents studied and worked in London. His foster parents encouraged him to perform, and he was greatly influenced by the pop music boom in London in the 1960s. Ogungbe's birth parents took him to Nigeria when he was nine years old, and from that time he became attracted to music from many different cultures. He took music lessons at Kings College Lagos in Nigeria, including violin lessons. By that time he was already creating his own music, as he could always hear tunes in his head. He also studied at the University of Ife in Nigeria, where he played in the ensemble for the first production of *Opera Wonyosi*, an update on *The Beggar's Opera* by Nigeria's Nobel Laureate, Wole Soyinka. Eventually he left the university to return to England to become a professional musician.

Back in England, Ogungbe took singing lessons and studied performance and communication skills at the Guildhall School of Music and Drama. He has composed for many groups, including several leading British theater and dance companies, as well as for his own music theater ensemble. Because he has worked with African musicians from a diverse range of backgrounds, as well as studied Western art music, his musical style often combines textures and **timbres** of various African instruments with those of Western orchestral and pop musical genres.

Timbre is the character or quality of a musical sound. It is the part of sound that allows us to hear the difference between a violin and a piano, or the difference between a voice and a West African fiddle.

1. Feeling the Pulse, 2014

Juwon Ogungbe (b. 1961, England/Nigeria)
Arranged and edited by Rachel Barton Pine

Feeling the Pulse
Composed 2014
Used by permission of the composer

Ignatius Sancho

Ignatius Sancho (1729–1780) was born on a slave ship off the coast of Guinea, West Africa, and was taken to the Spanish colony of New Granada in South America. When he was two years old he was brought to England. He grew up enslaved to three sisters in the town of Greenwich. Later, the Duke of Montague bought him. Despite being Sancho's enslaver, the Duke helped him learn to read and write. When he was older, the Montagues taught him literature, writing, and music. After the Duchess of Montagu died, Sancho was freed. He married and opened a small grocery store. He was probably best known as a public intellectual, publishing many letters about **abolishing** slavery. Sancho was also responsible for a number of important firsts. He was the first Black composer in history to ever have his music published. He wrote songs, minuets, and country dances and also published a book on music theory. He was also the first Black person to vote in a British election. When he died, he was the first Black person to have an obituary in the newspaper.

Abolish means to end a system or practice. Slavery was abolished in England and throughout the British Empire in 1833.

2. Les Contes des Fées, 1767

(Fairytales)

Ignatius Sancho (1729–1780, Guinea/New Granada/England)
Edited by Rachel Barton Pine

3. Le Vieux Garçon, 1767
(The Old Boy)

Ignatius Sancho (1729-1780, Guinea/New Granada/England)
Edited by Rachel Barton Pine

4. Minuet No. 15, 1770

Ignatius Sancho (1729-1780, Guinea/New Granada/England)
Edited by Rachel Barton Pine

BLACK ORCHESTRAS: FORGING ANOTHER PATH

There is a long tradition of symphony orchestras in the United States. The first professional symphony was the New York Philharmonic, which was established in 1842 and is still one of the most renowned orchestras in the world.

However, when the New York Philharmonic was created, it was still legal in many parts of the United States to own people as slaves. In fact, the enslavement of African Americans would be legal until 1865. Even after the legal **abolition** of slavery, it was difficult for Black Americans to participate in many aspects of broader American society. It was practically impossible to join an orchestra like the New York Philharmonic because of the creation of new laws that legalized **segregation** between White and Black Americans. Because of this widespread discrimination, many African Americans all over the country began their own societies, organizations, churches, and institutions. Classical music organizations were no exception. The existence of all-Black orchestras has been largely unrecognized in American history. However, a number of successful ensembles have left their mark.

> **Abolition** is the ending of a system or practice—the abolition of slavery in the United States happened in 1865 with the 13th Amendment to the Constitution.

> **Segregation** is the legal and/or social separation of people (based on differences like race, gender, and class). In addition to legal separation, segregation meant that many opportunities were unavailable to Black Americans, from swimming pool access to access to certain facilities, jobs and professions, neighborhoods, schools, and other institutions.

The earliest evidence of a Black American orchestra dates all the way back to the 1830s. The **Negro** Philharmonic Society was established in New Orleans around 1830 and consisted of over 100 musicians! But how could such a large orchestra exist in the early 1800s? Because of its unique history and the presence of many different populations and cultures, New Orleans had one of the largest populations of free Black people. Because they were free, many of the musicians could afford training on their instruments and spent time studying in Europe. At the same time, hundreds of miles north of New Orleans, the city of Philadelphia also had a significant population of free, upper-class Black people. Philadelphia

> **Negro** is a now outdated term used to describe African Americans from the 1700s through the mid-1900s. **Colored** is another outdated term used to reference African Americans.

composer and bandmaster Francis Johnson was the director of all-Black string and brass bands that often played classical music. In 1837, Johnson and one of his bands became the first American musical ensemble of any race to travel to Europe. Later, the all-Black Philadelphia Concert Orchestra was established in 1904, and eventually grew to be comparable in size with other major White American orchestras.

The Baltimore City **Colored** Orchestra made its debut in 1931 under the baton of Charles Harris. Decades later, the Civil Rights movement of the 1950s and 60s brought a renewed energy to provide opportunities for Black musicians. By the 1960s, several major orchestras that had previously been all-White hired their first Black members. The first African Americans who auditioned and won positions with major American orchestras include Donald White, Sanford Allen, and Ann Hobson Pilot. Donald White joined the cello section of the Cleveland Orchestra in 1957; Sanford Allen joined the violin section of the New York Philharmonic in 1962, 120 years after its creation; and Ann Hobson Pilot joined the Boston Symphony as a harpist in 1969.

In 1965, the Symphony of the New World was founded as an **integrated** orchestra, followed by the National Afro-American Philharmonic in 1978 and the Afro-American Chamber Music Society Orchestra in 1987. By the mid 1970s, after decades of widespread discrimination, the broader classical music world began to make efforts to include more African American musicians into their orchestras by creating fellowships. These fellowships gave qualified Black musicians and other musicians of color the opportunity to play with a professional orchestra for one or more years with the goal of training them for professional orchestra careers. Today, several orchestras still continue successful fellowship programs. Most orchestras also now hold auditions behind a screen so that judges cannot see the player's race, gender, age, weight, etc. to help ensure fair judgment of each musician's playing.

> **Integration** is the mixing of people of different races. An integrated orchestra is one that includes musicians of more than one race.

The Black orchestras mentioned so far no longer exist, but several successful Black orchestras and orchestras with inclusive missions created since the late 1980s continue to provide opportunities for Black musicians in the United States and Europe. These include the Chicago Sinfonietta, the Sphinx Symphony Orchestra, the Gateways Music Festival Orchestra, the Colour of Music Festival Orchestra, Orchestra Noir, and the Soulful Symphony. In 2015, the Chineke! Orchestra was founded in England and is the first orchestra of its kind in Europe.

Black orchestras have existed in the United States for almost 200 years, and their rich history will continue to influence classical music in the future.

—Danielle Taylor

Please visit www.musicbyblackcomposers.org/violin1 for a list of online and print resources that relate to this topic.

Estimated Racial/Ethnic Makeup of American Orchestras in 2014

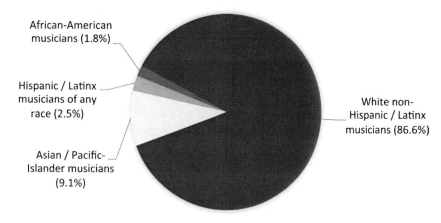

African-American musicians (1.8%)

Hispanic / Latinx musicians of any race (2.5%)

Asian / Pacific-Islander musicians (9.1%)

White non-Hispanic / Latinx musicians (86.6%)

Estimated Racial/Ethnic Makeup of the USA circa 2010

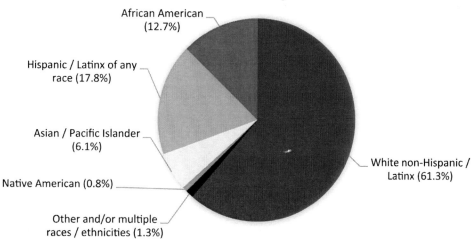

African American (12.7%)

Hispanic / Latinx of any race (17.8%)

Asian / Pacific Islander (6.1%)

Native American (0.8%)

White non-Hispanic / Latinx (61.3%)

Other and/or multiple races / ethnicities (1.3%)

Baltimore City Colored Orchestra

◢ Godwin Sadoh

Godwin Sadoh (b. 1965) is a Nigerian-American composer, instrumentalist, choral conductor, and scholar. He was born in the city of Lagos in the West African country of Nigeria, where he attended the Eko Boys' High School Lagos and sang in the school choir. He eventually became the school organist and choirmaster there when he was just 16 years old. After graduating, Sadoh directed several choirs and performed piano throughout Nigeria. He also studied piano, organ, music composition, and African music traditions in Nigeria before moving to the United States for advanced music study.

In the U.S., Sadoh earned a master's degree in ethnomusicology, specializing in African music; a master's degree in organ performance and church music; and a doctoral degree in organ performance and composition. This made him the first African to earn a doctoral degree in organ performance from any institution in the world. He is also the first Nigerian to earn a doctoral degree in music performance on any instrument. Sadoh composes for diverse musical ensembles and styles, and his music has been performed in Africa, Europe, North and South America, the Middle East, Asia, and Australia. He has taught at universities throughout the United States, and he has written scholarly articles on modern African art music, organ building, church music, and organist-composers in Nigeria.

5. Iya Ni Wura Iyebiye, 2001
(Mother is a Priceless Jewel)

Godwin Sadoh (b. 1965, Nigeria/USA)
Arranged and edited by Rachel Barton Pine

Iya Ni Wura Iyebiye
No. 2 from *Childhood Dreams for Piano*
Copyright 2015 by GSS Publications, Columbus, Ohio
Used by permission

Sister Marie-Seraphine Gotay

Sister Marie-Seraphine (Frances) Gotay (1865–1932) was born in San Juan, Puerto Rico. She left Puerto Rico when she was 17 and moved to New Orleans, where she joined the Sisters of the Holy Family and became a Catholic nun. At the **convent**, Sister Seraphine showed great musical abilities, and her superiors encouraged her to develop her talent. Her musical talent was so impressive that a local Catholic music school—which was ordinarily only open to White students—allowed her to study there. Sister Seraphine was a very curious and eager student, and so she learned to play almost every instrument! By the time she graduated, she could play strings, reeds, brass, percussion, harp, piano, and organ. She also composed, becoming the only Black woman composer known to be active in New Orleans at the turn of the 20th century.

Sister Seraphine composed a lot of music, but most of it was lost when the Sisters of the Holy Family moved their convent to a different neighborhood in the 1960s. "La Puertorriqueña: Reverie" is her only piece that still exists today. She also used her musical talents to improve the lives of children she taught. Sister Seraphine was in charge of music classes and the orchestra at the Sisters of the Holy Family's St. Mary's Academy in New Orleans, and she also gave music lessons to children at local orphanages. She even inspired a school band at St. Mary's Academy that is still in existence today!

A **convent** is a community of people devoted to religious life.

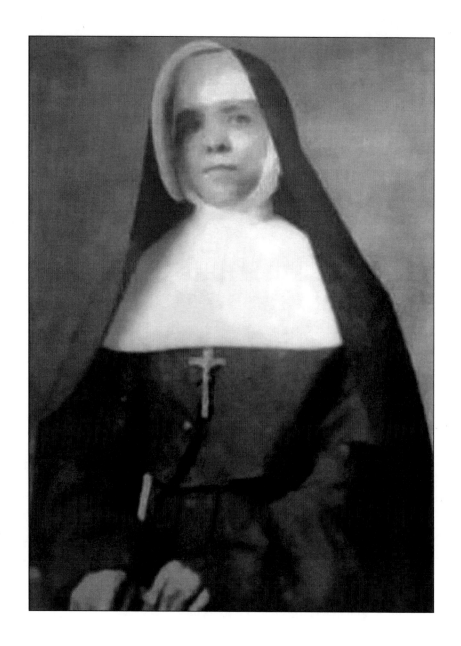

6. La Puertorriqueña: Reverie, 1896
(The Puerto Rican Woman)

Sister Marie Seraphine Gotay
(1865-1932, Puerto Rico/Louisiana)
Arranged and edited by Rachel Barton Pine

7. Just So in the North, 1767

Ignatius Sancho (1729-1780, Guinea/New Granada/England)
Edited by Rachel Barton Pine

Watch videos of Sphinx Soloist Program artists

Adé Williams

and Clayton Penrose-Whitmore
playing these pieces at
www.musicbyblackcomposers.org/violin1

Kenneth Kafui

Kenneth Kafui (ka-FOO-ee) (b. 1951) is a composer and teacher from the West African country of Ghana. He learned to play the **harmonium**, and he became the school organist at his high school where his father was also the music teacher. He later studied music at the University of Ghana in the country's capital city of Legon.

Kafui was guest composer for the Ghana Broadcasting Corporation Orchestra in 1978. He taught at the National Academy of Music in Ghanaian city of Winneba, and later became the conductor of the Ghana National Symphony Orchestra. In 1987, he received an award for best contemporary art music composer in Ghana. He is currently a lecturer in music theory and composition at the University of Ghana.

Recognized as one of the leading Ghanaian composers of his generation, he has written music for choir, orchestra, piano, organ, and for traditional African instruments. His music often includes Ghanaian rhythms, and his choral music often uses local Ghanaian languages.

The **harmonium** is a type of free-reed organ, which is lighter and more portable than pipe organs.

8. Mele Sue, 1986
(I am Young)

Kenneth Kafui (b. 1951, Ghana)
Arranged and edited by Rachel Barton Pine

Mele Sue
No. 2 from *Six Easy African Piano Pieces (Tonal)*
Copyright 1986, Ghana
Used by permission

ROLE MODEL PROFILE

Aaron Dworkin
Entrepreneur

Aaron Dworkin is the founder of the Sphinx Organization, a national arts organization dedicated to diversity in the arts. He is also a MacArthur Fellow (2005), a former member of the Obama National Arts Policty Committee, and President Obama's first appointment to the National Council on the Arts.

Mr. Dworkin: I was adopted when I was two weeks old by a white Jewish couple from Chicago. My parents were behavioral scientists—neuroscientists. Fast-forward 31 years, I was reunited with my birth parents: my birth father, who is a Black Jehovah's Witness, my birth mother, who is White Irish-Catholic. So I am all of that stuff all wrapped up into one. My adoptive mother was an amateur violinist. When I was five, she especially loved the old Milstein recording of the unaccompanied Bach, and she got reinvigorated by it. I really gravitated to it too, and so I started playing.

MBC: What was your life like as a young violin student?

Mr. Dworkin: Lots of practicing! Music and the violin for me is this incredible medium through which you can express, share, captivate, nurture, motivate, elucidate through your instrument. But you cannot do those things if you don't develop the ability to use it. That craft—the scales, the etudes—is so critical. If you do that to a level of excellence, especially when you're young, you have breadth of choices about what you then want to do with the instrument and with music. The way to do that is to practice, practice, practice.

MBC: What were your dreams and goals as a musician when you were a young person?

Mr. Dworkin: I thought I would win the Tchaikovsky Competition, and at the time I'd be the first American to win it, and the first African American or biracial American, and it would change the world! That was the big dream, but that didn't come to fruition. However, the way in which my life has unfolded professionally I far prefer to that. It was very interesting, when I first came to my parents with the idea of Sphinx, they said "what is this *mishegas* [the Yiddish word for 'craziness']? What are you doing? Just practice!" But three years into it they said, "you're having

more impact with this than you ever could have had, even if you would have become the world's greatest soloist." And so, you never know how your life will end up directing itself.

MBC: Tell me more about the Sphinx Organization. What was your motivation for founding it?

Mr. Dworkin: When I was a college student at the University of Michigan, in almost any musical circumstance, I was the only person of color, or one of less than a handful. But I never really thought about it all that much; I just knew it was my reality, and I was used to dealing with it. But I went into a lesson one day and my teacher Stephen Shipps said, "Do you want to play music by Black composers?" and I did not know at the time that there were any Black classical composers. It was a shock to me! He starts pulling these volumes of works off of his shelf: William Grant

Still, Roque Cordero, Joseph Bologne Saint-Georges. I'm like, "What? A contemporary of Mozart?!" I couldn't believe it. That, combined with going to concerts and not seeing many people of color on stage or in the audience, led me to an initial idea of: what if there was a competition for students like me? We could come together, play music by composers of color, and because we played that music, it would give visibility to that music. And through that process we would get scholarships, and if we did that: boom! Classical would be diverse within a couple of years! I soon realized it was much more complex a problem, but that was the initiation. And so things started with just the Sphinx Competition, and grew then into the entirety of the organization.

The Sphinx Competition is a competition for young Black and Latinx string players, with two divisions. The top prize winner of the Senior Division is a $50,000 artist award, and the top winners solo with 20 or 30 orchestras around the country. But now Sphinx is also much broader. It has a chamber orchestra that tours, it has summer programs, it has year-round educational programming, other things as well.

MBC: What were some challenges in terms of seeing Sphinx become a reality?

Mr. Dworkin: Funding is always a challenge. But one important thing is to try and find the ways you can move your mission forward that don't require money, and that helps you get a great distance. In-kind companies or organizations can share their facilities, and you build collaborations. Sphinx was built by—and is sustained through—vibrant collaborations and partnerships. It is partnerships that enable the winners to solo with a couple dozen orchestras throughout the year, that enable it to be broadcast on television and on radio to millions, that enable the students to all go to the top summer music programs, that enable Sphinx's own summer program. Partnering and collaborating are absolutely key.

MBC: What advice do you have for young violin students in general? And do you have any specific advice for students from a mixed-race or otherwise untraditional family background?

Mr. Dworkin: One of the things I say to Sphinx students is: Let Sphinx worry about the whole diversity thing. You practice. You become the best artist that you can be. There is no better weapon that you can

have in your arsenal—to overcome adversity, racism, prejudice, bigotry—than excellence. The core thing you need to bring in is a level of attentiveness to detail. They say that the difference between mediocrity and excellence is attention to detail. In music, the permissiveness for error is very, very limited. My former chamber music coach, Anthony Elliot, explained it like this: in sports, for instance, if you shoot more than 50% of your free-throws in, you're destined to be on one of the best teams. If you hit the ball more than 80% of the time, you're going to be a Hall-of-Famer. But if you play 95% of the notes right in the Beethoven Violin Concerto, people will want their money back. Excellence comes in the final 5% of what you do. So, when confronted with those issues of difference, approach them from that standpoint of excellence. If you're better, artistically, than everyone in the room, if you're smarter than everyone in the room, you diminish their ability to hurt you.

MBC: Now I have a couple of questions to just show that you're a real guy. What are some of your favorite pieces and composers?

Mr. Dworkin: First and foremost I have to say Bach. And specifically, even though I'm a violinist, the Cello Suites. I *wish* I could play the Cello Suites, because they are just simply outrageous; they're gorgeous; I

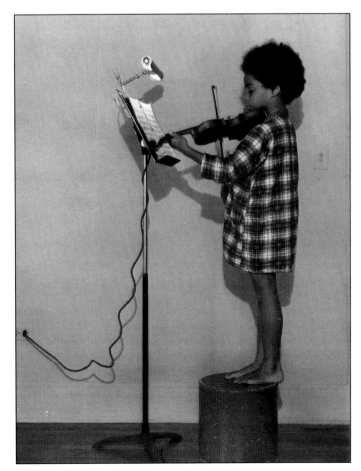

Young Aaron Dworkin practicing violin

never get tired of them. They are embedded in my DNA somehow. I have an affinity for the Bruch Violin Concerto. I'm sure I'm biased, because that was my debut when I was 13 years old, but I do love it. I love a lot of the work of William Grant Still. As an instrumentalist, I love the work of David Baker; I love some of the complexity, and in particular, I love his arrangement of Paganini. I love opera; I love *The Magic Flute* and *The Barber of Seville.*

But I also love hip hop. I absolutely love Tupac. I think he was an urban poet, an urban scribe. And I love blues. And when I'm driving, I love country. So I have an appreciation across the board. And depending on the mood, the situation I'm in, it will define what kind of music I'll listen to.

MBC: In the same vein, do you have anyone that you would consider to be your musical hero?

Mr. Dworkin: I'll take it one step further and say "human hero": Yo-Yo Ma. He is a beautiful player, obviously. But in addition to that, there is his sense for how his art connects with the rest of the world around him. And his generosity of spirit. When people are at that level of artistry, the sheer number of people you have to come in contact with, at some point you just have to shut off—wall yourself off—you just can't do it. But he somehow does it. He just gives. He's committed to young people. He's committed to how the arts intersect with our society. And so on any number of levels—artistry, humanity—Yo-Yo Ma is an inspiration.

Please visit www.musicbyblackcomposers.org/violin1 for a list of online and print resources that relate to MBC role models.

Sphinx Virtuosi 2016

9. Dutchess of Devonshire's Reel, 1779

Ignatius Sancho (1729-1780, Guinea/New Granada/England)
Edited by Rachel Barton Pine

Thomas Greene "Blind Tom" Wiggins

Thomas "Blind Tom" Wiggins (1849 – 1908) was born blind and enslaved near Columbus, Georgia, but he became one of the most famous American entertainers of the 1800s. The Bethunes, who enslaved Wiggins and his family, had seven children who played piano and sang, and young Wiggins loved to listen to their music. When he was still only four years old, he began to play back the music he heard on the piano. James Bethune could see that Wiggins was very talented, and so he paid for piano teachers for the boy. By the time he was eight years old, Wiggins was performing public concerts around Georgia, and eventually throughout the country, for the profit of Bethune. By the time he was 11 years old, he was already so famous that he became the first African American to be invited to perform for the president at the White House!

Wiggins likely was **autistic**, but that medical term did not yet exist to describe his behavior and skills. He had incredible abilities to remember and reproduce sounds. He could play back music on the piano that he had only heard once, play difficult classical pieces with his back turned to the piano, and could even perform three songs at once (one with his right hand, another with his left hand, and a third sung, each in a different key)! He also wrote his own music, which often used musical effects that mimicked sounds that he heard in his everyday life, like the sound of rain, the wind, and even a sewing machine.

Even though the end of the Civil War in 1865 should have freed all enslaved African Americans, the Bethunes found ways to keep legal and financial control of Wiggins. They kept all of the money he earned playing thousands of concerts. Even so, Wiggins was able to create music that was striking and unique. Listening to his music today, we can hear that Wiggins's creativity went farther than other composers would go until the middle of the 1900s.

Autistic is a term used for a person with autism. People with autism have certain unique ways of experiencing the world, and also sometimes have certain extraordinary skills.

BLIND TOM.
right 1880, by John G. Bethune.

10. The Boy with the Axles in His Hands, 1866

Thomas Greene "Blind Tom" Wiggins
(1849-1908, USA)
Arranged and edited by Rachel Barton Pine

11. Marianne's Reel, 1770

Ignatius Sancho (1729-1780, Guinea/New Granada/England)
Edited by Rachel Barton Pine

Horace Weston

Horace Weston (1825–1890) was an American composer and banjo player. He was born to free parents in Connecticut before the Civil War. He learned to play several instruments when he was a child. But he is most famous for playing the banjo, which he learned to play by ear when he was 30 years old. He became a **virtuoso** banjoist, and he played in popular theater performances of the day called **minstrel shows**. In fact, he became one of the biggest stars in minstrelsy in the mid-1800s!

In 1873, Weston toured Europe with a minstrel company that was performing *Uncle Tom's Cabin*. His performances there were highly praised, and he made history as the first Black performer to be featured in a special role. He was one of the first African-American musicians to become famous as a banjo player, and his style influenced many other musicians. He composed several pieces of music for banjo, including "The Birthday Party Waltz."

A **virtuoso** is a highly skilled musician.

Minstrel shows were an American form of entertainment that was popular in the 1800s and early 1900s. Minstrel shows included comic skits, dancing, and music that presented negative **stereotypes** about African Americans. At first, Black characters were played by White performers wearing black makeup. Later, Black people started performing in minstrel shows too. Even though minstrels portrayed Black people in negative ways, they were still one of the only ways for talented Black actors and musicians to perform professionally at that time.

A **stereotype** is a common but oversimplified image or idea of a particular type of person or thing.

Uncle Tom's Cabin is a book published in 1852 by the White American author Harriet Beecher Stowe, and it was also adapted into a stage play. The story presented African-American characters in disrespectful ways, but it also presented the horrors of slavery for White readers throughout the country. For this reason, it helped to spread anti-slavery ideas leading up to the Civil War.

12. The Birthday Party Waltz, 1883

Horace Weston (1825-1890, USA)
Arranged by Rachel Barton Pine and David Bontemps
Edited by Rachel Barton Pine

VIOLIN: AN INSTRUMENT OF BLACK LEADERS

We know that many Black people in history were famous professional violinists. For example, George Bridgetower was the professional violinist who inspired Beethoven to write his ninth violin sonata in 1803. But there are many other Black people who are well known for doing very important things in history, and who also played the violin as a personal passion rather than as a profession. For instance, did you know.....?

Solomon Northup was born in New York during the early 1800s. Unlike many other Black Americans at that time, Solomon was born as a free person. From his early years, he would spend his leisure time reading and indulging in his passion—playing the violin! He worked various types of jobs throughout the year, but during winter months when there wasn't as much other work, he would perform in different towns and villages for parties and dances. Through an unthinkable series of events, Solomon was kidnapped and sold into slavery, where he remained for twelve years. But even during the horrific circumstance of enslavement, Solomon never forgot his love of music. Even while he was enslaved, he had a reputation in the surrounding towns as a talented violinist, and was often sent to perform for parties and balls. When he had a few free hours on Sundays, he would go off and play his violin, because it provided him great comfort in harrowing times. As he later wrote, the violin was "an amusement which was the ruling passion of [my] youth . . . [and] the source of consolation since." He eventually gained his freedom and wrote about his experiences in a famous book, *Twelve Years a Slave*, and gave speeches about the need to end slavery.

Unlike Solomon Northup, **Frederick Douglass** learned to play the violin later in life. He was born in Maryland in the early 1800s and was **enslaved since birth**. However, he survived the horrors of slavery and eventually escaped to his freedom. As a free man, Frederick Douglass delivered many speeches and wrote essays about his life, including his memoir from 1845, *The Narrative of the Life of Frederick Douglass, an American Slave*. He became one of the most influential **abolitionists** of the 1800s. Because many people still wanted to recapture him into slavery, he traveled to Europe to remain safe. While he was in Scotland, he purchased a violin. As he got older, he would play songs and dances for guests and family members, and even played traditional **spirituals** to his grandchildren who sang and clapped their hands. One grandchild, Joseph Henry Douglass, grew up to enjoy a successful career as a professional violinist—and even performed for two presidents! Today, Frederick Douglass's violin sits on display at the Frederick Douglass National Historic Site near Washington, DC.

> In many states, children of enslaved women were automatically enslaved.
>
> **Abolitionists** are people who work to end slavery.
>
> **Spirituals** are a type of religious song associated with Black Christians of the southern United States. Spirituals are believed to be first created by enslaved Africans before the end of the Civil War by combining European hymns (religious songs) with African musical elements.

Frederick Douglass's violin

George Washington Carver is another important African American who was also born into slavery. Thankfully, when George was only one year old, the Civil War came to an end and the slavery of African Americans was abolished. The couple who had owned him, Moses and Susan Carver, decided to raise George and his brother James as adopted sons. Susan taught George to read and write; Moses was a well-known fiddler, and George also learned to play his violin. He loved to learn, and when he grew up,

Engraving of Solomon Northrup, circa 1853

Frederick and Joseph Douglass

George found colleges and universities that would allow Black students to enroll. He had played guitar, accordion, piano, fiddle, and took singing lessons; his singing teacher and her husband urged him to go to college and study music, and so he studied art and music at Simpson College in Iowa. But his main passion was science! He went on to study __botany__ at Iowa State, where he was the first Black student in the university's history. He later taught at Tuskegee Institute, and became a scientist and inventor. His discoveries about farming and plants (especially

Botany is the science of plants.

peanuts) helped improve the lives of struggling farmers, including many other African Americans who had once been enslaved. The George Washington Carver National Monument at his birthplace in Diamond, Missouri honors his life and work, and his violin is on display there.

In the 1900s, it became easier for African Americans to formally study music. One of the most well-known Civil Rights era leaders, **Coretta Scott King**, was a person who took advantage of these opportunities. She began violin as a child, and went on to study music in college. In the 1950s, she earned a degree in voice and violin from the prestigious New England Conservatory of Music. However, a few years later, her path changed after she met and married Dr. Martin Luther King, Jr. Together they fought for justice and equality for African Americans throughout the country. They raised four children together, and Coretta Scott King kept music in their lives, as the family played violin and piano and sang together.

Sheila Johnson is an entrepreneur and philanthropist who has made achievements in hospitality, sports, TV/film, the arts, education, women's empowerment, and community development. Most famously, she co-founded the Black Entertainment Television (BET) network in 1979. This groundbreaking station changed the landscape of American television by promoting diverse images, stories, and entertainment by and for African Americans. But before she co-founded BET, Sheila Johnson was a violinist and music teacher. She began to study the violin at age nine, and when she was in high school she became the first African-American woman to become the concertmaster of the Illinois All-State Orchestra. She later studied at the University of Illinois where she graduated with a degree in music education. After that, she and her husband moved to Washington, DC, where she worked as a music teacher and managed her own private violin studio. At the height of her career as a violin teacher she had 100 students, and went on several international tours with them. Her students even performed for the King and Queen of Jordan! Managing a successful music studio helped her develop many of the skills that she would need to create and manage a company like BET, and achieve her many other impressive accomplishments.

Perhaps the public figure with the most recent public debut is **Minister Louis Farrakhan**, who became the spiritual leader of the Nation of Islam in 1978. He learned violin as a child, but eventually was asked by his spiritual teacher to choose between his music and his religious duties. In 1993, after a nearly forty-year pause, Minister Farrakhan dusted off his instrument, practiced, and performed the Mendelssohn concerto with an orchestra in North Carolina. This performance was conducted by Maestro Michael Morgan, a prominent African-American conductor and Artistic Director of the Oakland Symphony.

When we remember these important African Americans we think of their great strength, their work for racial equality, and their leadership for their communities. It is also exciting to know that the violin was an important part of their lives, bringing joy to themselves and to all of those who heard their music.

—Danielle Taylor

Please visit www.musicbyblackcomposers.org/violin1 for a list of online and print resources that relate to this topic.

13. Mele Ekpom, 1986

(I Do See It)

Kenneth Kafui (b. 1951, Ghana)
Arranged and edited by Rachel Barton Pine

Mele Ekpom
No. 4 from *Six Easy African Piano Pieces (Tonal)*
Copyright 1986, Ghana
Used by Permission

Watch videos of Sphinx Soloist Program artists

Clayton Penrose-Whitmore

and Adé Williams

playing these pieces at

www.musicbyblackcomposers.org/violin1

Felipe Gutiérrez y Espinosa

Felipe Gutiérrez y Espinosa (1825 – 1899) was born in San Juan, which is the capital city of the Caribbean island of Puerto Rico. He became one of the first classical composers born on the island, and the most important Puerto Rican composer of operas and religious music in the 1800s.

Gutiérrez studied music with his father, who was a Spanish musician, but he was mainly self-taught. As a young man, he became a musician in the army, and when he was 20 years old he was the bandmaster of his battalion. When he was older, Gutiérrez earned the post of choirmaster of the San Juan Cathedral, where he stayed for forty years. He also conducted for a time at the Teatro Tapia (then called the Teatro Municipal), which is a theater that was the center of cultural life in San Juan for over 100 years.

Throughout all of these years, Gutiérrez was a very active composer. He wrote the first operas in Puerto Rico, as well as a great deal of religious music. He also ran a free music school so that he could teach and share music with anyone who wished to learn.

14. La Despedida, 1800s

(The Farewell)

Felipe Gutiérrez y Espinosa
(1825-1899, Puerto Rico)
Arranged and edited by Rachel Barton Pine

Thomas J. Martin

Thomas J. Martin (1800s) was an American composer who was active in New Orleans, Louisiana in the mid-1800s. There is not any information about Martin's childhood in historical records, and very little about his adulthood either. We do know that he published many pieces between 1854 and 1860, and that he was a free man of color in the years before the Civil War.

He played the guitar and the piano, and he operated a large teaching studio in New Orleans for many years.

"Had I Never Never Known Thee" was Martin's most popular song, and it was published at least ten times in the 1800s!

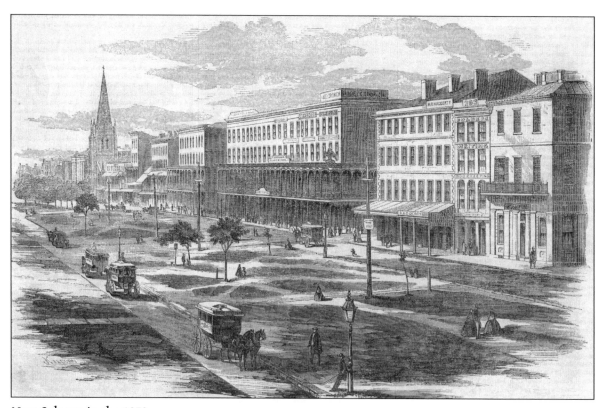

New Orleans in the 1850s

15. Had I Never Never Known Thee, 1858

Thomas J. Martin (19th century, New Orleans)
Arranged and edited by Rachel Barton Pine

Joseph Bologne, Chevalier de Saint-Georges

Joseph Bologne, <u>**Chevalier de Saint-Georges**</u> (1745–1799), was born on the island of Guadeloupe in the Caribbean, the son of an enslaved woman and a French plantation owner. Saint-Georges moved with his parents to France when he was six years old. When he was 13, he began fencing lessons and he quickly became one of the most famous swordsmen in Europe. His early musical training was in school, but in his early 20s, he studied privately with the well-known French composer Joseph-François Gossec. Saint-Georges soon became the concertmaster of Gossec's orchestra. He made his solo debut at 27 when he played his first two violin concertos with them.

Saint-Georges became an influential composer in his day. Along with his teacher, he was one of the first composers in France to write string quartets, and his symphonies concertantes for two violins and string orchestra inspired Mozart. Saint-Georges also worked as a conductor. He directed the Amateurs, which quickly became one of the most famous orchestras in Europe. He also founded his own orchestra in 1781. Under his direction, this new orchestra premiered Joseph Haydn's six Paris Symphonies. When the French revolution started, Saint-Georges joined the National Guard and became a colonel, leading an entire combat regiment. As he got older, Saint-Georges changed from composing instrumental music to writing operas. At the end of his life, he was still conducting concerts to great acclaim.

Chevalier is Joseph Bologne's title, which means "Knight." It was also common in France to name people according to their home town, and so "**de Saint-Georges**" means "from the town of Saint-Georges." Joseph Bologne became so famous that he is usually referred to as simply the Chevalier de Saint-Georges because so many people knew him by that title. Imagine a violinist from Detroit growing up to become so famous that everyone called them the Violinist of Detroit!

16. Theme from Sonata No. 4 for Two Violins, ca. 1780s

Joseph Bologne, Chevalier de Saint-Georges
(1745-1799, Guadeloupe/France)
Edited by Rachel Barton Pine

Francisca "Chiquinha" Gonzaga

Chiquinha (she-KEEN-ya) Gonzaga (1847–1935) was born and lived in Rio de Janeiro, which is one of the biggest cities in the South American country of Brazil. Her full name was really Francisca Edwiges Neves Gonzaga, but people throughout Brazil call her by the affectionate nickname "Chiquinha" because she became such an important and beloved composer, pianist, and conductor in their country. Gonzaga received a very good education, including in music, and she wrote her first composition at age 11.

When she was 16, Gonzaga married a businessman chosen by her family. But their marriage was not happy, and her husband did not want Gonzaga to have a musical career. She left her husband and asked for a divorce. This was a great scandal at the time and caused her family to reject her. She married a second time, but again divorced, and so she had to make money and support herself and her children. This was a great challenge for a woman in the 1800s, since women were expected to marry and serve their husbands and families. Gonzaga was able to make money as a piano teacher and a performer, and she eventually became successful as a composer. She wrote over 2,000 pieces throughout her lifetime, including the music for 77 musical plays. In 1885, she also became the first woman in Brazil to conduct an orchestra.

17. Balada, 1884

Francisca "Chiquinha" Gonzaga (1847-1935, Brazil)
Arranged and edited by Rachel Barton Pine

ROLE MODEL PROFILE

Lucinda Ali-Landing
Suzuki Teacher ——————————————
Founder-Director of the Hyde Park Suzuki Institute (HPSI)
Orchestral Player and Freelance Violinist

Lucinda Ali-Landing is a violinist and Suzuki teacher in Chicago. In addition to directing and teaching at the HPSI, Ms. Ali-Landing performs as a freelance violinist, as well as in the Illinois Philharmonic Orchestra and Chicago Sinfonietta. She lives in the South Shore with her husband and four lovely children.

MBC: Please tell me about how you started playing the violin.

Ms. Ali-Landing: My dad's a violinist (later switched over to viola), and I remember listening to him practice at three o'clock in the morning, every day, just practicing. And one day I said, "Oh, I'd like to play the violin!" and my very next memory was having a violin, and him giving me lessons. He taught me the first year.

MBC: Did you have any other friends that played the violin?

Ms. Ali-Landing: Nope. Not really. It was just my sister and me. My sister's a cellist. I grew up on the Southwest Side of Chicago. Once we went into youth symphony, as teenagers, we met some people that we became friends with from our neighborhood, but mainly everybody thought we were either crazy or nerds or... [Laughter] mostly just nerds...

MBC: At what point did you decide to make your life in music?

Lucinda Ali-Landing and her father

Ms. Ali-Landing: Well my life *was* music until I quit at the end of my Bachelor of Violin Performance degree. I went to Northern Illinois. But I quit the violin 'cause I was tired of practicing, and I didn't even really know about careers. I don't think anybody had embraced me and said, "This is what you can do and this is what's possible." I just wanted a job, so I quit and went into social services. But then I decided that I did want to continue playing, so I took an audition with Illinois Philharmonic. Afterward they left a message on my machine, and it said that I did not get in, which was not typically what happened! When I took an audition, I got in! So when they said, "You didn't make it," I was thinking, "What? What did you just say? I didn't hear you properly." [Laughter] I was just devastated, so I decided to start taking lessons again. I called Mark Zinger at DePaul and begged him to take me into his studio and he actually encouraged me. I think that was the first non-family member who encouraged me. I was in my early twenties.

MBC: A big part of your professional life is teaching. When did you first start teaching others?

Ms. Ali-Landing: I started teaching in undergrad at a local school that was in our town. But I started teaching little children in graduate school. I was really hungry, decided I needed to eat, so I decided to get whatever the popular certification was at that time—it was Suzuki—and started teaching children. I got a teaching job and I didn't know anything about children. There are not a lot of children in our family, and so I just did not have a lot of experience with children. So I just went in and I enjoyed the first child I taught so much, and I just loved teaching children.

MBC: What is it that you especially enjoy about teaching kids?

Ms. Ali-Landing: I enjoy creating something from scratch. I enjoy teaching a child who's excited to know, and giving them the information, watching them just kind of work it out, bringing it back to you. It's something you can mold, and just something you can create. It's almost like a piece of art.

MBC: Wonderful. Now, at a certain point you decided to take the plunge and start your own school...

Ms. Ali-Landing: I was teaching as a director of the young violinists over at the Sherwood Conservatory, and I wanted to bring something like what I was doing there south of 13th and Michigan. So, I chose Hyde Park, and started with ten students in 1998. We're having our 20th anniversary in the '18-'19 season.

MBC: Wow! And how much has it grown? How many students attend now?

Ms. Ali-Landing: We have about 75 families—there are lots of siblings. Everybody gets a private lesson, a repertoire class, a theory class, chamber music when they're ready, or Music in Movement if they're little kids. But we're small now. We're looking at our business model again this year and we'll go into 2019 doing something different.

MBC: How is the experience you're giving your students different from your experience growing up?

Ms. Ali-Landing: Well, one of the things that we've created is a community. The parents and the children interact inside and outside of the institute. Our children played together when they were small, they went over to each other's houses. The musical school has always functioned like a family in a community. And those early people are still my personal friends. We raised our children together, and watching parents be Suzuki parents helped me be a mother. Those people became the community in which my children still exist today.

MBC: Violin is not just a supplement, but a part of their core lifestyle. And your work is not separate from your kids.

Ms. Ali-Landing: That's been it for the past 17 years. My children have come to work with me every single day for the past 17 years. In fact, there was not a moment when they were not what I consider musicians. I homeschool them, and I started educating them as infants, and not just music. In other things too.

MBC: Do you have advice for a kid who loves to play the violin and music, but doesn't like to practice?

Ms. Ali-Landing: It's way easier to love when you know how to play it! [Laughs] You have to put in the hard work, just like everything else, if you want to get the enjoyment out of it.

MBC: Do you enjoy any other kinds of music other than classical?

Ms. Ali-Landing: I love gospel music, jazz, I do like rap and R&B, yep, I sure do... I like everything. I grew up on country western; I know all the songs. If you name one, I could sing it. [Laughs]

MBC: What are your goals and dreams and ambitions?

Ms. Ali-Landing: Well, since we already talked about the school, I'll say part of my personal mission is to give excellent, excellent instruction, so if children decide they want to be professional when they're whatever age, they can audition and go to whatever school they want to—they'll have the skill-set to do that, especially African-American children. And before when I auditioned it was like I'm the only African American there. When I'm 55 years old and still auditioning, I want to see at least 30 other African Americans there, because ya know, it's a numbers game. The more people show up, the more chances that somebody's going to get an orchestra job. So

Lucinda Ali-Landing with students

that's one of my personal wishes in life. I'd like to play with the Lyric. [Laughter] That's a nice, cushy job... So as far as performing, just lots of chamber music, playing some good music and being able to live a nice lifestyle by having people enjoy my music.

MBC: And what advice do you have for kids or for their parents who are starting violin lessons and just learning what it's all about?

Ms. Ali-Landing: I don't have any advice for children. I have advice for the parents. Don't let your children quit. Commitment—if you start, see it all the way through, 'til they are all the way grown. Because they are going to want to quit, you know, every other month, and they will just have wasted your money. I've never heard an adult say, "I am so glad my parents let me quit and now I don't know how to play the piano." I always hear, "I wish they would not have let me quit and I would know how to play the piano by now." So, I would just say to the parents that the benefits outweigh the struggles. And commit to it— make them brush their teeth, eat their vegetables, and practice. [Laughter]

Please visit www.musicbyblackcomposers.org/violin1 for a list of online and print resources that relate to MBC role models.

Lucinda Ali-Landing with her daughters

Clarence Cameron White

Clarence Cameron White (1880–1960) was an American composer and violinist who was born in Clarksville, Tennessee. He began learning violin when he was eight years old. His teachers were violinist and composer Will Marion Cook and the violinist Joseph Douglass. White wrote his first composition when he was 12. It was a piece for violin and piano. When he was 16, he went to the famous Oberlin Conservatory in Ohio. He got his first job as a teacher at the Washington, DC Conservatory after he finished his studies. White went to England twice to study with the Afro-English conductor and composer Samuel Coleridge-Taylor.

White was considered to be one of the best violinists of his day. But during his lifetime, Black soloists were still almost always excluded from playing in or soloing with White orchestras, and Black orchestras were few and far between. Determined to perform, White frequently gave concert tours throughout the United States with his wife, Beatrice Warrick White, accompanying him on the piano. His compositions were often influenced by **spirituals** and African-American folk music. Famous violinists like Fritz Kreisler and Jascha Heifetz recorded his pieces *Bandana Sketches* and "Levee Dance" from *Concert Paraphrases of Traditional Negro Melodies, Op. 27, No. 4*, but White was best known for his dramatic works. Some of his operas were performed in Carnegie Hall and the Metropolitan Opera House in New York City. In 1919, White helped found the National Association of **Negro** Musicians. This group is the oldest African-American music organization in the country, and it is still active today.

Spirituals are a type of religious song associated with Black Christians of the southern United States. Spirituals are believed to be first created by enslaved African Americans before the end of the Civil War by combining European hymns (religious songs) with African musical elements.

Negro is an outdated term used to reference African Americans that was mainly used from the 1700s through the mid-1900s.

18. Tuxedo, 1895

Clarence Cameron White (1880-1960, USA)
Violin 2 arranged by Rachel Barton Pine

54

Amadeo Roldán y Gardes

Amadeo Roldán y Gardes (1900–1939) was a composer, violinist, conductor, and teacher. His parents were from the Caribbean country of Cuba. He was born in Paris and grew up in Europe, where he began to play the violin when he was five years old. When he was eight, he entered the Conservatory of Madrid in Spain, where he began to study composition in addition to violin. He graduated from the conservatory when he was 16 years old, but continued studying music with famous teachers in Spain for a few more years.

When Roldán was 21, he moved to Havana, Cuba, where he lived for the rest of his life, and he became a leader of cultural activities in the city. He was the conductor and music director of the Havana Philharmonic Orchestra. He also founded the Havana String Quartet, and became a professor of composition and director of the Havana Municipal Conservatory. In 1959, the school was renamed the Amadeo Roldán Conservatory in memory of Roldán.

During his years in Cuba, Roldán was very important in bringing new life to concert music on the island. His compositions use Afro-Cuban rhythms, and he was the first composer to bring features of Black Cuban folklore and culture into concert halls. He did this by finding creative ways to mix Afro-Cuban music with contemporary European concert music styles. Roldán's life was short, but his ideas and music continue to an inspiration for other Cuban musicians and composers.

19. Canción de Cuna Del Niño Negro, 1937
(Lullaby for a Black Child)

Amadeo Roldán y Gardes (1900-1939, France/Cuba)
Arranged and edited by Rachel Barton Pine

Canción de Cuna Del Niño Negro

Basile Jean Barès

Basile Barès (1846 – 1902) was an American composer who was born in New Orleans, Louisiana. His father was a French carpenter and grocer, and his mother was an African-American woman enslaved by a man who owned a music and piano store. Since his mother was enslaved when he was born, Barès was also enslaved from birth. He grew up working in his enslaver's music store, which is where he probably first learned to play the piano and began to compose. He eventually took piano and composition lessons, and was very skilled at a young age. In fact, he wrote "Grande polka des chasseurs à pied de la Louisiane" when he was only 16 years old. What is even more amazing is that this is the only American piece that was published and given copyright protection to an enslaved composer!

Like other enslaved African Americans, Barès was made legally free at the end of the Civil War in 1865. But he continued to work at the same music store, which was then owned by his former enslaver's widow. He traveled to Paris on business for the store, where he also played piano at the Paris International Exposition in 1867.

Back in New Orleans, Barès had become a well-known pianist. He often played with other **Creole** musicians, and was involved in movements to help **desegregate** music venues in the city. He was so well-regarded that he was often hired to play for Carnival balls for members of the White community, where he also led a **string band**. He stayed active as a composer, and had many more of his own compositions published for several decades after the Civil War.

In New Orleans and the Caribbean, the word **Creole** is used to describe people of mixed racial ancestry, usually including French or Spanish and African heritage.

To **desegregate** is to end the practice of keeping people of different races separate.

String bands are ensembles made up of mainly string instruments. Different from orchestras, they often include banjos, guitars, and other plucked instruments in addition to bowed string instruments like the fiddle. In the late 1800s, string bands played popular folk music styles, and later string bands also played jazz.

Original cover of Barès's "Grande Polka des Chasseurs à Pied de la Louisiane," published in 1860

20. Grande Polka des Chasseurs à Pied de la Louisiane, 1860
(Louisiana Infantrymen's Grand Polka)

Basile Jean Barès (1846-1902, New Orelans)
Arranged and edited by Rachel Barton Pine

ROLE MODEL PROFILE

Tai Murray
Solo Violinist
Chamber musician

Tai has soloed all over Europe and North America with orchestras like the Chicago Symphony, the BBC Symphony in England, and the Philharmonic Staatsorchester of Mainz in Germany. She has also released several CDs of European and American music.

MBC: Please tell me about where you grew up and how you got started playing violin.

Ms. Murray: I'm from Chicago, and my mother tells me that I asked to play the violin when I was really, really young. Since I was so little, at first my family thought I wasn't serious—a little girl saying, "I want to play the violin," just like, "I want to be a fireman," or, "I want to be an astronaut." But I really meant it! My aunt said that when I was very young, she walked into a room and I was alone standing right in front of the television. And she asked, "Why are you standing there like that?" And I said, "Can't you see?! There's a violin!" So apparently, I was really *all* about it.

When my mother realized I really was serious about it, she decided to find me a teacher. I started with a Suzuki teacher. But since my mother was also an elementary school teacher, she felt I had to learn to read music too. So I studied with a more traditional teacher at the same time. I also studied at the Music Center of the North Shore in Chicago.

My mom and brother and I moved from Chicago to Bloomington, Indiana when I was eight. My mom discovered that Indiana University has a very good conservatory. I was able to get an incredible education there. I was also able to keep going to the Music Center of the North Shore thanks to my grandmother. She still lived in Chicago, and she made two round trips to Bloomington every single weekend driving me back and forth. She made so many sacrifices so that I could continue to go to Saturday class at the Music Center of the North Shore, and later the Midwest Young Artists.

MBC: When you were traveling so much, do you remember how much you were practicing, or how you felt about practicing in your younger years?

Ms. Murray: I started studying with Yuval Yaron in Bloomington. He was a very demanding teacher. A real musician. A real artist. He didn't normally

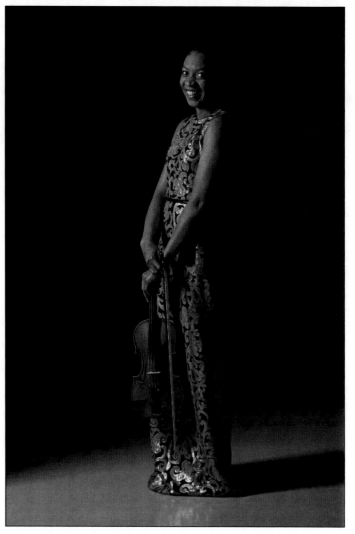

teach children, and so if I wanted to study with him as a child, he required me to really practice. I don't remember *always* enjoying it. I'm sure I learned serious lessons about responsibility, of course. But I don't remember that I ever had to be forced to practice. I just liked to do *that* more than anything else. And after fourth grade I was home-schooled, and so my practicing was incorporated into my day. It probably varied from three hours to not more than six. Since my mother was an educator, she was aware that it is possible to hurt yourself doing something too much. And so she kept me from going overboard with it.

People ask me that now, "How much do you practice?" And I don't know, I just have my violin in my hand all the time! That's what I do. It's always been more than a job. It's always been *in* my life. I had some inspiring teachers and music coaches throughout my life. I remember there was a teacher during the early times I was in Indiana. His name was Rostislav Dubinsky, and he was one of the founding members of the Borodin Quartet. I remember him saying to me, "Make sure you practice. You *have* to work." And he wasn't saying it because I *wasn't* practicing. He was saying it because he thought, "You seem like you want to *do* this. So if you want to do this, this is what it takes."

MBC: You came upon people who were already titans in the classical music world when you were so young. Do you remember any of your musical influences when you were growing up?

Ms. Murray: Yes, definitely all my teachers. Brenda Wurman, Ron Levy, Susan Rozendaal, Mimi Zweig, Yuval Yaron, Franco Gulli. Those were all my teachers. I also studied with Shmuel Ashkenasi and Henry Kowalski. And then there were the people were sort of just outside that circle: Josef Gingold, Leonard Hokanson, Yorgi Chebak, János Starker, Miriam Fried, Nelli Shkolnikova—basically all of those people who were in Indiana.

MBC: When was your first opportunity to solo with an orchestra, and what was that like for you?

Ms. Murray: That was before we moved from Chicago. I think I was seven. The first time I ever played with an orchestra, I played with the Chicago Youth Symphony with Michael Morgan conducting. And then a year later I played with the Chicago Symphony, also with Michael Morgan conducting at Orchestral Hall. And I liked playing with the orchestra. I have memories of enjoying that. But one of the big things I also remember was my mother saying, "You will not be some kind of child star. You will not be a child masquerading as an adult." And so there was never any extra pressure. She taught me that the preparation is more important than the concert. And I remember

literally walking off stage and going into the dressing room to sit on the floor to play Legos with my brother. So it never became a stressful thing. I think that as a result, to this day, I look forward to walking out on stage. I don't have nerves. Of course I have adrenaline, but I don't have any trepidation. I don't have stage fright. I think that goes back to the beginning when my mother said things like, "There will be no extra pressure. No trying to be a child star." I appreciate that now as an adult.

As I got older, my mother would also say, "If at any time you decide you don't want to do this, that is just fine." She would never say something like, "Don't let me see you stopping." No, no, no. She said, "This is all your decision. If you want to be a violinist, then *do* that. And if you do, then you have to work. You have to be responsible, have dedication. But if you decide this is not what you want to do, that's also fine." And that's also stuck with me.

MBC: That's fantastic. So, what advice would you give to young violin students and aspiring musicians?

Ms. Murray: That's a hard one, because everyone is so individual, and everyone is coming from a different place. But I would say, in the modern world, having a job is important. If you want to actually *work* as a musician, you should know who you are before you go for that job. Finding a job in any field can be frustrating. For instance, you hear a lot of actors say they hear a lot of "nos" before they finally hear that one "yes" that starts their career. But they go through all those "nos" because they're sure they want to be an actor. So you have to be sure you want

to be a musician so that you're able to withstand anything negative that might happen. So I guess that's my advice: Know who you are as a musician. Have that core before you branch out to your other goals.

MBC: Can you remember your most memorable musical experience, whether it's as an audience member, or being on stage, or making music with other people?

Ms. Murray: Really, I've just had too many to condense it to one. It isn't really possible. I've had great experiences as an audience member. I've had incredible experiences on stage as a performer. I think for me, the next performance is the most important. So you can think back on great experiences playing concerts, but even though I had that experience, it has *nothing* to do with the concert tomorrow, in a way. You have to let it go. Whether it was good or bad, it's gone, it's in the past. There's no changing it, and there's no holding onto it. And so, I think, being able to say, "Time for the future," is, in a way, the most gratifying thing about being a professional performer. The focus shifts to the next performance, always.

MBC: Thank you for taking the time to talk with me! Do you have any final words to share?

Ms. Murray: "Long live descriptive music!" We call it "classical music" because that's an easy way of referring to it. But technically classical music is Mozart, more than 200 years ago. We've come a *long* way, so the term doesn't actually apply! So I call it "descriptive music." Because it's not necessarily meant to make you dance, though it can. But it's more of an intellectual dance. So I think of "descriptive" as something that engages the mind, and an emotional state, in a way that perhaps other kinds of music don't try to do. And so that is my closing statement: Long live descriptive music!

Please visit www.musicbyblackcomposers.org/violin1 for a list of online and print resources that relate to MBC role models.

Scott Joplin

Scott Joplin (1867 or 1868–1917) was an American composer, performer, and teacher best known for writing a style of music called **ragtime**. He grew up in a town called Texarkana on the border of Texas and Arkansas. When he was a child, many members of his family played musical instruments, and so he also became interested in music. When he was a young man, Joplin worked as a touring musician, and later published his many compositions. He did not like the usual publishing contracts, and so in 1899 he hired a lawyer before publishing any more music. This was a very good idea because his next publication, "Maple Leaf Rag," was extremely popular and sold half a million copies within 10 years, earning Joplin a steady income. "Maple Leaf Rag" became the most famous of all piano rags, and Joplin was called the King of Ragtime Writers.

Joplin also wanted to write for the theater, and he eventually wrote a ballet and two operas. One opera was lost, but the other one, which was called *Treemonisha*, he published himself in 1910. *Treemonisha* was not performed in its entirety during his lifetime, and Joplin's music was mostly forgotten for many years after he died. But it became popular again in the late 1900s, when it was featured in new concert programs, opera productions, recordings, a movie soundtrack (*The Sting*, 1973), music festivals, television commercials, and more. In 1975, *Treemonisha* was fully staged on Broadway for the first time. In 1976, Joplin received a special **posthumous** Pulitzer Prize.

Ragtime is a style of popular music characterized by syncopation and often played on the piano. It was created by Black American musicians in the late 1890s.

A **posthumous** award is one that is given after the winner has died.

21. The Entertainer, A Ragtime Two-Step, 1902

Scott Joplin (1867-1917, USA)
Arranged and edited by Rachel Barton Pine

Will Marion Cook

Will Marion Cook (1869–1944) was an American composer, conductor, and violinist. He was born in Washington, DC and went to live with his grandparents in Chattanooga, Tennessee when he was ten years old. His musical talent was clear very early, and he was sent to study the violin at Oberlin College Conservatory when he was 15. He was supported there by his mentor, the important **abolitionist** Frederick Douglass. Douglass helped to raise money to send Cook to study in Europe, and so he spent two years in Berlin, Germany. Back in the United States, Cook helped promote Black American music and musicians through **Colored** American Day (August 25, 1893), an event that was a part of the World's Columbian Exposition in Chicago. Later, he attended the National Conservatory in New York where he studied with the famous Czech composer, Antonín Dvořák. However, he suffered constant discrimination as a classical performer, and so he eventually became discouraged and turned to popular theater music. His unique classical music background allowed him to help create a new type of popular song for Black American musical comedies at the turn of the 20th century.

Abolitionists are people who work to end slavery.

Colored is a now outdated term used to describe African Americans.

People gather at the World's Columbian Exposition in Chicago in 1893

Statue of Columbia at the World's Columbian Exposition in Chicago in 1893

22. Chocolate Drops
A Cake Walk, 1902

Will Marion Cook (1869-1944, USA)
Arranged and edited by Rachel Barton Pine

SOURCE NOTES

1. JUWON OGUNGBE
Feeling the Pulse

Original instrumentation	voice and piano
Original key	G major
Year composed	2014
Publisher	N/A (unpublished)
Portion	excerpt

2. IGNATIUS SANCHO
Les Contes des Fées (Fairytales)

Original publication	*Minuets Cotillons & Country Dances for the Violin, Mandolin, German Flute, & Harpsichord, Composed by an African*
Original instrumentation	treble line and bass line
Original key	F major
Year published	ca. 1767
Publisher	London, "Printed for the Author"

3. IGNATIUS SANCHO
Le Vieux Garçon (The Old Boy)

Original publication	*Minuets Cotillons & Country Dances for the Violin, Mandolin, German Flute, & Harpsichord, Composed by an African*
Original instrumentation	treble line and bass line
Year published	ca. 1767
Publisher	London, "Printed for the Author"

4. IGNATIUS SANCHO
Minuet 15

Original publication	as Minuet 9 in *Minuets etc. etc. for the Violin, Mandolin, German Flute, and Harpsichord, Composed by an African, Book 2nd*
Original instrumentation	treble line and bass line
Year published	1770
Publisher	"London. Printed for the Author and sold by Richard Duke at his Music Shop near Opposite Great Turn-stile Holborn, where may be had Book first"

5. GODWIN SADOH
Iya Ni Wura Iyebiye (Mother is a Priceless Jewel)

Original publication	No. 2 from *Childhood Dreams for Piano*
Original instrumentation	piano
Original key	F major
Year published	2015
Publisher	GSS Publications, Columbus, OH
Portion	excerpt

6. SISTER MARIE SERAPHINE GOTAY
La Puertorriqueña: Reverie (The Puerto Rican Woman)

Original instrumentation	piano
Original key	A flat major
Year published	1896
Publisher	Junius Hart, New Orleans
Portion	excerpt

7. IGNATIUS SANCHO
Just So in the North

Original publication	*Minuets Cotillons & Country Dances for the Violin, Mandolin, German Flute, & Harpsichord, Composed by an African*
Original instrumentation	treble line and bass line
Year published	ca. 1767
Publisher	London, "Printed for the Author"

8. KENNETH KAFUI
Mele Sue (I am Young)

Original publication	No. 2 from *Six Easy African Piano Pieces (Tonal)*
Original instrumentation	piano
Year published	1986
Published in	Ghana

9. IGNATIUS SANCHO
Dutchess of Devonshire's Reel

Original publication	*Twelve Country Dances for the Year 1779*
Original instrumentation	treble line and bass line
Year published	1779
Publisher	Paul's Church Yard, London

10. THOMAS WIGGINS
The Boy with the Axles in his Hands

Original publication	*Blind Tom's Vocal Compositions*
Original instrumentation	voice and piano
Year published	1866
Publisher	Root & Cady, Chicago

11. IGNATIUS SANCHO
Marianne's Reel

Original publication	*Minuets etc. etc. for the Violin, Mandolin, German Flute, and Harpsichord, Composed by an African, Book 2nd*
Original instrumentation	treble line and bass line
Year published	1770
Publisher	"London. Printed for the Author and sold by Richard Duke at his Music Shop near Opposite Great Turn-stile Holborn, where may be had Book first"

12. HORACE WESTON
The Birthday Party Waltz

Original instrumentation	two banjos
Year published	1883
Publisher	S.S. Stewart, Philadelphia

13. KENNETH KAFUI
Mele Ekpom (I Do See It)

Original publication	No. 4 from *Six Easy African Piano Pieces (Tonal)*
Original instrumentation	piano
Year published	1986
Published in	Ghana

14. FELIPE GUTIÉRREZ Y ESPINOSA
La Despedida (The Farewell)

Original instrumentation	voice and piano
Year published	1921
Publisher	Silver, Burdett and Company, Boston

15. THOMAS J. MARTIN
Had I Never Never Known Thee

Original instrumentation	voice and piano
Year published	1858
Publisher	P.P. Werlein & Co., New Orleans
Portion	first verse only

16. JOSEPH BOLOGNE, CHEVALIER DE SAINT-GEORGES
Theme from Sonata No. 4 for Two Violins

Original publication	*Six Sonatas for Violin*
Original instrumentation	two violins
Year published	1800 (posthumous)
Publisher	Ignace Pleyel, Paris
Portion	Theme from *Sonata No. 4*, second movement

17. CHIQUINHA GONZAGA
Balada

Original publication	from the operetta *A Corte Na Roça (The Court at Roça)*
Original instrumentation	voice and piano
Year composed	1884
Publisher	Acervo Digital Chiquinha Gonzaga (revised edition 2011)
Portion	first verse only

18. CLARENCE CAMERON WHITE
Tuxedo

Original instrumentation	violin and piano
Year published	1895
Publisher	Henry White, Washington, DC

19. AMADEO ROLDÁN
Canción de Cuna Del Nino Negro (Lullaby for a Black Child)

Original instrumentation	piano
Year published	1937/1941
Publisher	unknown Cuban/Carl Fischer, Inc.

20. BASIL BARÈS
Grande Polka des Chasseurs a Pied de la Louisiane (Louisiana Infantrymen's Grand Polka)

Original instrumentation	piano
Original key	A flat major – E flat major
Year published	1860
Publisher	J. Tolti & D. Simon, Lith. 115, Exchange Alley, New Orleans, LA
Portion	all except opening 16 measures

21. SCOTT JOPLIN
The Entertainer, a Ragtime Two Step

Original instrumentation	piano
Year published	1902
Publisher	John Stark & Sons, St. Louis, MO
Portion	excerpt

22. WILL MARION COOK
Chocolate Drops, a Cakewalk

Original publication	No. 14 from *In Dahomey, A Negro Musical Comedy*
Original instrumentation	piano
Year published	1902
Publisher	Keith, Prowse & Co. Ltd., London
Portion	excerpt

CREDITS

BOOK CREDITS
Executive Editor and Music Editor: Rachel Barton Pine
Managing Editor, Head Researcher and Writer: Dr. Megan E. Hill
Contributing Writer: Danielle Taylor
Contributing Arrangers: David Bontemps, Jason Moy, and Dr. Carlos Simon
Cover Artwork: JUJOcreative

MP3 CREDITS
Rachel Barton Pine, violin
Matthew Hagle, piano
Violin: "ex-Bazzini ex-Soldat" Guarneri del Gesu, Cremona, 1742
Strings: Vision Titanium Solo by Thomastik-Infeld
Bow: Dominique Pecatte
Piano: Steinway D
Piano Technician: Christa Andrepont
Session Producer: Jim Ginsburg
Post-Session Producer: Rachel Barton Pine
Engineer: Bill Maylone
Recorded December 30, 2017 in the Fay and Daniel Levin Performance Studio at 98.7 WFMT, Chicago, Illinois

PHOTOGRAPHY CREDITS

The publisher and editor would like to thank the following people, museums, libraries, and other institutions for permission to reproduce their material. Every care has been taken to trace copyright holders. However, if we have omitted anyone we apologize and will, if informed, make corrections in any future edition.

t = top, c = center, b = bottom, l = left, r = right

Cover graphic design by JUJOcreative; MBC Composers Collage **cover&4l-r**, Samuel Coleridge-Taylor, public domain; Chevalier de Saint-Georges, etching by Ward from the oil painting by Mather Brown, 1788, printed with permission of the Archive dépt. de Guadeloupe; J.H. Kwabena Nketia, courtesy of J.H. Kwabena Nketia; Florence Price, courtesy of Special Collections, University of Arkansas, Fayetteville; Roque Cordero, courtesy of the Cordero family; Jessie Montgomery, courtesy of Jessie Montgomery; **5** photo by Lisa-Marie Mazzucco, courtesy of Rachel Barton Pine; **6t** photo by Dr. Sarah Moncada, courtesy of Dr. Megan E. Hill; **6b** photo by the University of Michigan, courtesy of Dr. Mark Clague; **7t** photo by Guy Edouard Cesar, courtesy of David Bontemps; **7b** photo by Jacen Paige, courtesy of Dr. Carlos Simon; **8** photo by Ally Almore, courtesy of Danielle Taylor; **10** photo by Crispin Hughes, courtesy of Juwon Ogungbe; **12** by Francesco Bartolozzi, published by John Bowyer Nichols, after Thomas Gainsborough, stipple engraving, published 2 July 1781 (1768), courtesy of the National Portrait Gallery Picture Library of the UK; **17b** public domain, courtesy of the Peabody Institute Archives, Johns Hopkins University; **18** courtesy of Dr. Godwin Sadoh; **20** courtesy of the Society of the Holy Family; **23** photo by Glenn Triest, courtesy of the Sphinx Organization; **24** courtesy of Kenneth Kafui; **26** photo by Kevin Kennedy, courtesy of Aaron Dworkin; **27** photo by Barry Dworkin, courtesy of Aaron Dworkin; **28** photo by Kevin Kennedy, courtesy of the Sphinx Organization; **30** public domain, 1880, Library of Congress, LC-USZ62-84287; **33** public domain, HTC Photographs 1.1073, Houghton Library, Harvard University; **36l** public domain, from Solomon Northup, *Twelve Years a Slave*, (Auburn: Derby and Miller, 1853); **36r** photo by Carol M. Highsmith, courtesy of the National Park Service, Museum Management Program and the Frederick Douglass National Historic Site (FRDO 2505); **37** public domain, photo by Denis Bourdon, 1894, courtesy of the Collection of the Smithsonian National Museum of African American History and Culture, Gift of Dr. Charlene Hodges Byrd; **39** photo by Glenn Triest, courtesy of the Sphinx Organization; **40** public domain; **42** public domain, from *Ballou's Pictorial* 13 no. 5 (August 1, 1857), from a pencil drawing by Mr. Kilburn, from a photo by James Andrews; **44** etching by Ward from the oil painting by Mather Brown, 1788, printed with permission of the Archive dépt. de Guadeloupe; **46** public domain; **48t** courtesy of Lucinda Ali-Landing; **48l** courtesy of Lucinda Ali-Landing; **49b** courtesy of Lucinda Ali-Landing; **50** photo by Paul Elledge, courtesy of Lucinda Ali-Landing; **51** public domain, from Maud Cuney-Hare, *Negro Musicians and Their Music* (Washington, DC: The Associated Publishers, Inc., 1936): 329; **55** public domain; **58** public domain, from Rodolphe Lucien Desdunes, *Nos Hommes et Notre Histoire*, (Montréal: Arbour & Dupont, 1911), facing page 164, printed with permission of the Louisiana State University Libraries; **59** public domain, from Basile (Barès), *Grande Polka des Chasseurs à Pied, de la Louisiane* (New Orleans: J. Tolti & D. Simon, 1860); **62** photo by Gaby Merz, courtesy of Tai Murray; **63** Tai Murray, *20th Century: The American Scene*, Ashley Wass on piano, CD, Easonus, EAS 29253, 2013; **64** photo by Gaby Merz, courtesy of Tai Murray; **65** public domain; **68** public domain, from Maud Cuney-Hare, *Negro Musicians and Their Music* (Washington, DC: The Associated Publishers, Inc., 1936): 132; **69t** public domain, 1893, Library of Congress, LC-USZ62-97300; **69b** public domain, 1893, Library of Congress, LC-USZ62-102149.

SUPPORT MUSIC BY BLACK COMPOSERS
by purchasing cool merchandise
with distinctive MBC logos!

https://www.cafepress.com/musicbyblackcomposers

ALSO AVAILABLE!

RACHEL BARTON PINE FOUNDATION

LudwigMasters PUBLICATIONS

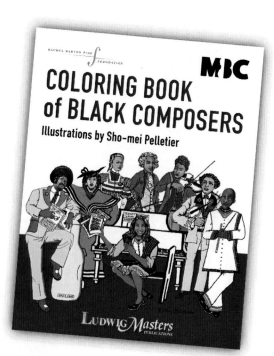

The Rachel Barton Pine Foundation
Coloring Book of Black Composers
#55300001

The first of its kind, this book honors 40 remarkable international Black classical composers from the 1700s to the present day. Each vivid illustration is accompanied by a biography that puts his or her life and music into historical perspective.

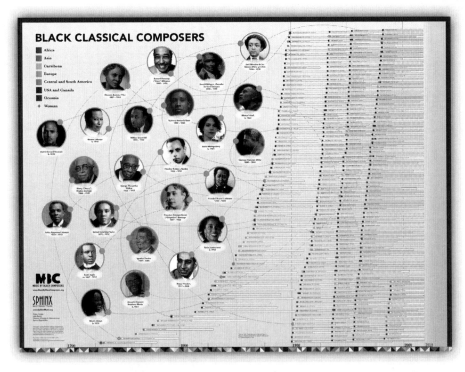

Black Classical Composers Timeline Poster (25 x 33½ in.)
#55900001

Created in partnership with the Sphinx Organization, this poster features the names of more than 300 composers from around the world, including men and women from the 1700s to the present day, and indicates the countries and regions in which they lived and worked.

This educational resource demonstrates the depth and breadth of Black classical music making throughout history, and is a colorful and engaging addition to any music or general education classroom, music studio or practice room, or children's play space.

LudwigMasters Publications
11221 St Johns Industrial Pkwy North • Jacksonville, FL 32246
(800) 434-6340 • (561) 241-6169 • Fax: (561) 241-6347 • www.ludwigmasters.com